Toilets Timeline

ca. 3000 BCE

Stone houses at Skara Brae, Scotland, have toilet "cells" with drains underneath.

ca. 200 BCE

Chinese farmers build pigsty toilets.

1596

Sir John Harington publishes a description of a flushing toilet, in England.

ca. 2000 BCE

Egyptians use clay pots filled with sand. In many lands, pots are used as indoor toilets for the next 4,000 years.

ca. 2600 BCE

Mohenjo-daro (Pakistan) and nearby cities have stone box toilets and sewers.

ca. 500 CE

First recorded use of toilet paper, in China.

ca. 400 BCE–400 CE

Romans build public toilets and huge underground sewers.

1880s

Factories mass-produce cheap, clean flushing toilets in Europe and the United States.

1830s

First public lavatories built, in France.

2011

The Gates Foundation in the United States funds "Reinvent the Toilet" challenge to help provide more toilets worldwide— and save lives.

1850–1900

Professional plumbers in Europe and the United States design new toilets, tanks, and flushing devices.

1775

Alexander Cummings invents S-bend trap to stop smells.

1980

Automatic high-tech "washlet" toilet invented in Japan.

What Happens When You Flush?

1. Pushing the handle down pulls the piston up.

2. As the piston moves up, it pushes water into the siphon.

3. Water flows through the siphon (up one side and down the other) and down into the toilet bowl.

4. The water swirls around the toilet bowl, mixes with solid or liquid waste, and flows out of the waste pipe.

5. As the tank empties, the float ball (which floats on top of the water) moves downward.

6. As the float ball moves down, it pulls down a rod attached to the inlet valve. This lets water flow into the tank from the inlet pipe. Slowly, the tank fills with water again.

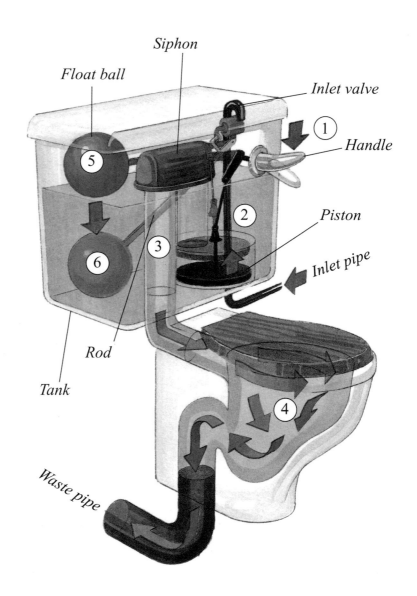

Float ball · Siphon · Inlet valve · Handle · Piston · Inlet pipe · Rod · Tank · Waste pipe

The modern siphonic flush toilet system is based on a design invented by British plumber George Jennings in 1854. For over 100 years, it was the only design allowed in the UK, because it did not waste water.

In bowl-siphon toilets, popular in the United States, the bowl can only be emptied when a large amount of water flows into it very quickly. This fills a siphon tube at the base of the bowl, which then sucks all the water and waste away.

Author:

Fiona Macdonald studied history at
Cambridge University and at the University of
East Anglia, both in England. She has taught adult
education, and in schools and universities, and is
the author of numerous books for children on
historical topics.

Artist:

David Antram was born in Brighton, England,
in 1958. He studied at Eastbourne College of Art
and then worked in advertising for 15 years before
becoming a full-time artist. He has illustrated many
children's nonfiction books.

Series creator:

David Salariya was born in Dundee,
Scotland. He has illustrated a wide range of books
and has created and designed many new series
for publishers in the UK and overseas. David
established The Salariya Book Company in 1989.
He lives in Brighton with his wife, illustrator
Shirley Willis, and their son, Jonathan.

Editors: Stephen Haynes,
Caroline Coleman

Editorial Assistant: Mark Williams

PAPER FROM
SUSTAINABLE
FORESTS

© The Salariya Book Company Ltd MMXV
No part of this publication may be reproduced in whole or in
part, or stored in a retrieval system, or transmitted in any form or
by any means, electronic, mechanical, photocopying, recording,
or otherwise, without written permission of the publisher. For
information regarding permission, write to the copyright holder.

Published in Great Britain in 2015 by
The Salariya Book Company Ltd
25 Marlborough Place, Brighton BN1 1UB

ISBN-13: 978-0-531-21215-8 (lib. bdg.) 978-0-531-21306-3 (pbk.)

All rights reserved.
Published in 2015 in the United States
by Franklin Watts
An imprint of Scholastic Inc.
Published simultaneously in Canada.

A CIP catalog record for this book is available
from the Library of Congress.

Printed and bound in China.
Printed on paper from sustainable sources.

1 2 3 4 5 6 7 8 9 10 R 24 23 22 21 20 19 18 17 16 15

SCHOLASTIC, FRANKLIN WATTS, and associated logos are
trademarks and/or registered trademarks of Scholastic Inc.

You Wouldn't Want to Live Without™

Toilets!

Written by
Fiona Macdonald

Illustrated by
David Antram

Created and designed by
David Salariya

Franklin Watts®
An Imprint of Scholastic Inc.
NEW YORK • TORONTO • LONDON • AUCKLAND • SYDNEY
MEXICO CITY • NEW DELHI • HONG KONG
DANBURY, CONNECTICUT

Contents

Introduction

I t's a strange shape: a seat with a hole, or maybe just a hole with footrests. It's smooth and shiny, cold and hard. It's often bright and white, though it may be stainless steel or even softly colored.

We've all seen it; we've all used it. It's a comfort, a convenience—essential for cleanliness, and a sign of progress. Without it, towns and cities could not function and travel would be difficult. It's probably the biggest lifesaver the world has ever seen.

But we don't talk about it much, and, if we have one, we usually keep it hidden. What is it? Yes, of course you've guessed! It's the humble, necessary toilet—and it has a long and fascinating history.

Read on, and find out more. And think! How would you like to live without a toilet?

My hero!

Could You Cope Without a Toilet?

In just one year, the average adult produces 133 gallons (503 liters) of urine and 353 pounds (160 kilograms) of feces (solid waste). A child produces a little bit less, because he or she is smaller.

With a world population of around 7 billion, there's an awful lot of pee and poop needing to be disposed of. Most is flushed away down toilets—though, sadly, over 2 billion people in poor or war-torn lands still do not have toilets, running water, or proper drains.

Today, in many places, it's against the law to build a house without a toilet. But, until the 20th century, even royal palaces went without them. So how did people in the past keep clean and comfortable? How did they cope without toilets?

Where is it?

LONG AGO, people used just about any place as a toilet. But peeing or pooping in public was not always safe or simple...

Top Tip

Don't go in the snow! Early Arctic explorers dug toilet holes in the snow—and found that their pee turned instantly to ice! Ouch!

BEHIND A BUSH. What's lurking here? You might get a nasty surprise!

UNDER A TREE. Falling fruit could knock you out—with your pants down!

IN A DARK CORNER. Aargh! It's full of creepy-crawly critters!

Begone, thou ill-bred lout!

IN A FIELD. Not all farm animals are friendly—watch out!

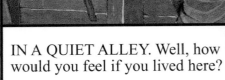

IN A QUIET ALLEY. Well, how would you feel if you lived here?

IN THE GARDEN. No! Gardens ought to smell sweet!

IN THE SEA. Wild waves might knock you over and sweep you away, forever!

7

You'd Find It Unhealthy...

If you could travel back in time, you'd soon see that life without toilets was messy, smelly, and unhealthy. Many dangerous bacteria lurked in pee and poop (together called sewage), ready to infect men, women, and children. But no one knew for certain that bacteria cause disease until French scientist Louis Pasteur proved it in 1862. Before then, people believed that "miasmas" (bad smells from sewage) brought many different kinds of sickness. So they did not understand how dangerous sewage could be—especially if mixed with drinking water. As a result, epidemics (mass outbreaks of disease) brought death and terror to Europe, Asia, and America.

Killer Cholera

LONDON, ENGLAND, 1854. Here's a terrible real-life example of what polluted water can do. Sewage dripped from piles of human waste and trickled deep underground.

THE SEWAGE was full of bacteria that caused a disease called cholera. It mixed with underground water that was later pumped up to the surface—for Londoners to drink!

ALMOST EVERYONE who drank that water caught cholera. They became horribly, horribly sick and had terrible diarrhea.

BEWARE! FLIES AREN'T PICKY! That's how they spread disease. They suck up sewage from toilets and heaps of waste…

…then spit some out onto nice, fresh, clean food, to help them digest it! Ugh! How revolting!

I don't feel so well now…

THOSE WHO CARED for the sick often became ill themselves.

DEATH IN A DROP. In 1855, London doctor John Snow suggested that cholera was spread by dirty water.

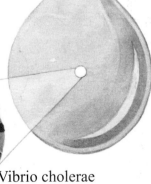

SEWAGE FROM SICK PEOPLE was thrown away and seeped down into the soil, filling the underground water with still more deadly bacteria.

CHOLERA KILLED—AND QUICKLY! Thousands of Londoners died from cholera within just a few days. Doctors were powerless to save them.

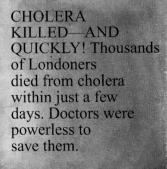

Vibrio cholerae *bacteria*

SNOW WAS RIGHT: A single drop of water can carry almost a million cholera bacteria.

...and So Would the Environment!

Sewage can be bad for wildlife as well as for people. When most families lived in the countryside, a little sewage spread on farmland did not do much harm. In fact, some farmers plowed it into their fields to feed their crops and help them grow. This was safe, so long as the farm produce was thoroughly washed or cooked before it was eaten.

THE GREAT STINK. In 1858, sewage in the River Thames smelled so bad that many Londoners ran away from the city. Engineer Joseph Bazalgette built huge new underground drains to take sewage safely out of the city.

Leading politician Benjamin Disraeli calls for action to end the Great Stink.

But, as towns and cities grew bigger, vast quantities of sewage produced by the people who lived there were dumped on the surrounding land or spilled into rivers. It polluted the water, poisoned fields, killed local plants and animals, and destroyed natural ecosystems.

ROTTING SEWAGE gives off a gas called methane. It can cause huge explosions, and it contributes to global warming.

METHANE BUBBLES may catch on fire when they make contact with oxygen in the air, and glow with an eerie light. In the past, people said these lights were ghosts, which they called jack-o'-lanterns or will-o'-the-wisps.

Will-o'-the-wisp

Top Tip

Never use a "flying toilet"! That's the nickname for a plastic bag used as a toilet and then thrown away. It's disgusting for anyone who finds it, dangerous for wildlife, and pollutes the environment.

Would You Dig – or Get a Pig?

People in the past may not have understood how dangerous sewage could be, but they still didn't like its smell or messiness. So they tried to find ways of managing pee and poop to make life cleaner and more pleasant. Even Stone Age hunters, 10,000 years ago, set aside corners of their camps to use as middens (waste heaps). Around 1000 BCE, Hebrew shepherds looked for private spots at a decent distance from their tents, dug little holes, then covered their waste with earth. Simple—and clean and tidy. And in ancient China, almost 2,000 years ago, farmers invented a clever way of using pigs to dispose of their sewage. Recycling waste has a very long history!

WILD WOLVES scavenged around Stone Age hunters' camps, eating waste—and sewage. After many years the wolves became tame. Our modern dogs are descended from them.

TWICE AS CONVENIENT. Build your toilet above your pigsty, like ancient Chinese farmers did. This will mean free food for your animals—and more pork for your family.

Pottery model of a pigsty toilet, made in China around 200 CE

13

Top Tip

Want to wipe? Use dried grass, or moss, or leaves, or rounded shells (careful!). If possible, wipe with your left hand, so that your right hand stays clean to use for eating.

Go With the Flow

Holes in the ground or pigsty toilets were fine for country folk, but once large numbers of people began to live close together in cities, a new way of managing sewage was needed. Poor people made do with pots, in their houses or on street corners. But the rich and powerful wanted to keep their fine city homes clean and sweet-smelling. So, in many different civilizations, from the Indian subcontinent to ancient Greece and Rome and the far north of Scotland, engineers built houses with indoor toilets. The best toilets were linked to channels flowing with water that would carry sewage away.

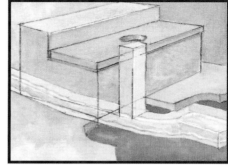

IN MOHENJO-DARO (built ca. 2600 BCE, now in Pakistan) wealthy families had stone box toilets, cleaned by running water.

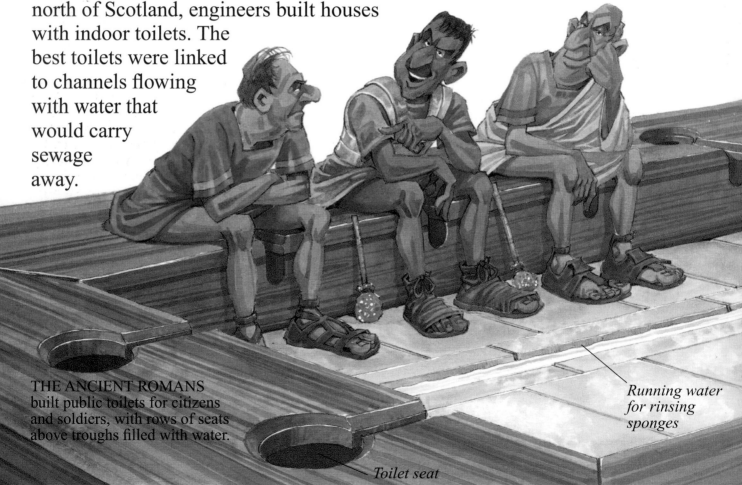

THE ANCIENT ROMANS built public toilets for citizens and soldiers, with rows of seats above troughs filled with water.

Running water for rinsing sponges

Toilet seat

AT SKARA BRAE (built ca. 3000 BCE on the Orkney Islands of Scotland), village homes had stone "cells" with drainage ditches underneath, so sewage could trickle outside.

Top tip

Keep standing! Don't sit down, like the Romans did—stand or squat instead. Squatting's the tradition in many lands, especially in Africa and Asia. And doctors say it's better for your bowels!

Yes, that's the toilet!

COULD YOU SHARE a sponge on a stick? Or wipe with a bit of broken pottery? That's what Roman soldiers used for toilet paper. Wealthy Romans preferred goose feathers—tickly!

TAKE A TRIP—if you can stand the smell—along the Cloaca Maxima (built ca. 600 BCE), Rome's great underground sewer. It carries waste from city buildings to the river, and is big enough for inspectors to row their boats right through it.

Could You Cope With a Chamber Pot or Clean a Cesspit?

Who'd Be a Gong Farmer?

You're a poor city dweller in England in the 1500s. You've filled your clay-pot toilet. Now what? If you're lazy and dirty, you might just empty it out the window, with no respect for passersby. Eventually, the rain will wash the sewage away, but not before you've made the street slimy, slippery, and smelly. If you're a bit more thoughtful, you might dig a cesspit in the yard behind your house. Or you could use the public cesspit. But cesspits fill up and need emptying—and that's not always easy.

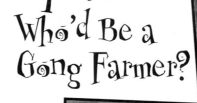

1. AS A GONG FARMER, you empty cesspits, which is possibly the worst job in the world!

2. FIRST, YOU DIG UP the sewage and shovel it into a cart. It's exhausting!

3. THEN YOU DRIVE the sewage out to the country. You must do this after dark, because the sight and smell are so disgusting.

SINKING INTO THE SEWAGE? GET PATTENS— wooden overshoes that lift your shoes high above the muck of the streets.

5. WORST OF ALL, you get bitten by rats, flies, and fleas. They carry nasty diseases, and so does the sewage. Sooner or later you'll get sick and die!

4. YOUR FRIENDS can't bear to be near you. You stink! You're wet! You're filthy!

Would You Prefer Somewhere Private?

If you met a boy from 16th-century England and he said he was going to "the privy," would you understand him? Perhaps you could guess? *Privy* means "private," and it was a polite name for a toilet. Similarly, we often say we're going to "the bathroom" or "the restroom," even though we don't intend to take a bath or to rest.

Going to the toilet is natural. Everyone does it. But in many past societies— just like today—polite, well-bred people thought it was rude or shameful to talk in public about toilets, drains, or sewage. For the same reason, they liked to go to the toilet in a very private place, and invented lots of different ways of doing that.

Oh, to Be Alone!

HIDE YOUR BLUSHES behind a movable wicker screen, as the Vikings did (ca. 800–1100 CE). Viking toilets were just holes in the ground. When full, they were covered over and a new hole was dug nearby.

EDINBURGH, Scotland, ca. 1500: You can pay to crouch over a wooden tub with a cloak draped around your shoulders for privacy.

"GARDEROBE" was a polite word for a medieval toilet. It also means a clothes cabinet. Sometimes toilets were built next to cloakrooms in the hope that toilet smells would keep moths away from the clothes.

Castle wall *Stone seat* *Chute*

Top Tip

Don't copy 17th-century Londoners, who built cesspits right next to their cellars. Waste could—and did—seep through walls and floors, into neighbors' houses.

GOT A GARDEN? Build an "outhouse"! It's a little wooden hut built over a small private cesspit.

TOILETS ON SHIPS, called heads, are holes in the sides of the hull, fitted with seats for privacy—and safety. Try not to face into the wind…

18TH-CENTURY DINERS passed around a pot under the dinner table.

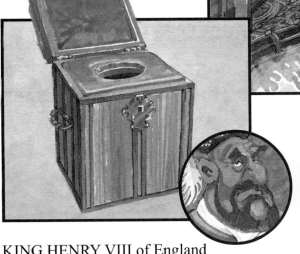

KING HENRY VIII of England (ruled 1509–1547) chose a close-stool: a bucket hidden in a velvet box trimmed with gold and ribbons.

SIT ON A BOURDALOUE! It's said to have been named after a French priest famous for very long sermons.

VICTORIAN FAMILIES concealed chamber pots for nighttime use in tidy little bedroom cupboards.

Flushed With Pride

People in the past made good use of water power. They built watermills to grind corn or operate heavy hammers. They even measured time with water clocks. But no one thought of bringing water indoors and using it to flush toilets until the young English poet Sir John Harington (1561–1612) had a very bright idea. He added lead pipes flowing with water to a storage tank (called a cistern), and joined them to a closestool fixed over a drain. This was the first private indoor toilet that could flush away sewage.

BEFORE HIS TIME? Around 1589, Harington proudly installed the world's first flushing privy in his house in the country. But his invention was ignored for almost 200 years.

HARINGTON'S PRIVY. To work the toilet, pull the top plug (b) so water flows from the tank (A) into the toilet bowl (D). Pull the lower plug (f) to open a flap (K) in the pipe to let sewage flow away.

You Can Do It!

Ask an adult how you can save precious water when flushing the toilet. There are several possible ways, such as putting a brick in the tank so that it holds less water.

And Her Majesty doesn't much like your poems either.

FIT FOR A QUEEN? Harington built a second privy as a gift for his godmother, Queen Elizabeth I (ruled 1558–1603). But she did not use it. Courtiers said that she did not like the noise it made.

Driven Around the Bend

Around 1700, as towns and cities grew larger, so did the problem of sewage. Old-fashioned cesspits were still used in some places until 1900. So were little backyard privies filled with earth, ash, or sand. However, beginning in the 1850s, after deadly epidemics and horrible smells, city governments began to make strict new laws to manage sewage. All new city houses had to have a toilet flushed by flowing water, and be connected to underground drains that carried sewage away.

STAND IN LINE! In poor city districts, a single backyard toilet is shared by several families. It's soon full—and overflowing!

Brick box (has to be emptied)

Earth, ash or sand

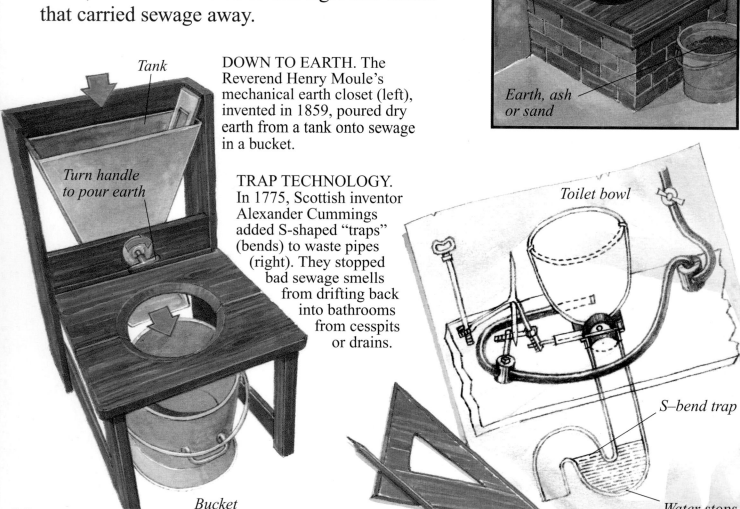

Tank

Turn handle to pour earth

DOWN TO EARTH. The Reverend Henry Moule's mechanical earth closet (left), invented in 1859, poured dry earth from a tank onto sewage in a bucket.

TRAP TECHNOLOGY. In 1775, Scottish inventor Alexander Cummings added S-shaped "traps" (bends) to waste pipes (right). They stopped bad sewage smells from drifting back into bathrooms from cesspits or drains.

Toilet bowl

S–bend trap

Water stops smells.

Bucket

BLOCKED DRAINS could make sewage bubble back up into toilet bowls! Thomas Crapper's new underground drains were easier to keep clean.

English plumber Thomas Crapper (1836–1910)

Inspection cover in sidewalk

Cutaway view of underground chamber

Blocked pipe can be cleared here

It's a good old English name. It means "harvester."

Dolphin, 1880

Lion, 1896

Garlands of flowers, ca. 1890

ARE YOU SITTING COMFORTABLY? From around 1880, toilet bowls were mass-produced in factories, together with cisterns, bathtubs, and hand basins. These stylish products are from the famous Twyford factory in the English Midlands.

Sitting Pretty

In addition to building new drains, city leaders also planned safe new water supplies.

Starting around 1850, big underground pipes known as water mains carried clean, fresh water beneath city streets, ready to flow into kitchens and bathrooms. Professional plumbers, such as Thomas Crapper, invented new "siphonic" cisterns, so water from the mains would not be wasted. A full cistern held only enough water to flush sewage down the drain, but no more. Floating ball valves controlled water flowing in to refill cisterns, and also stopped water flowing back from cisterns into the mains.

FOR MORE INFORMATION, see the diagram near the front of this book.

Lever   Piston   Float ball

SIPHONIC ACTION. Cisterns are operated by a chain attached to a lever and piston.

Siphon

PULLING THE CHAIN forces the water up into a tube called a siphon. The siphon sucks the water down to gush into the toilet bowl below.

Whoosh!

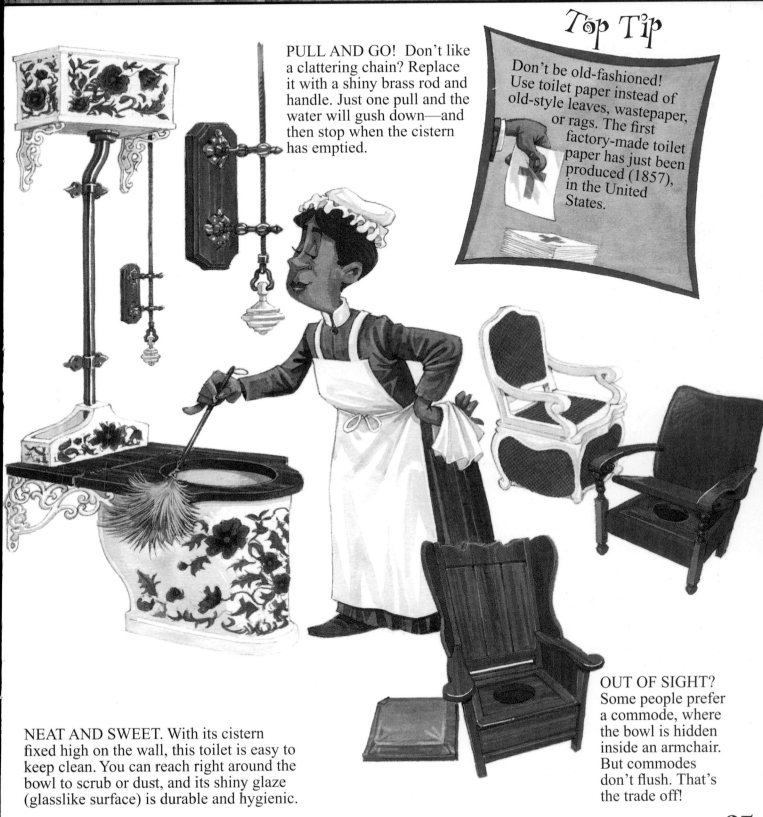

PULL AND GO! Don't like a clattering chain? Replace it with a shiny brass rod and handle. Just one pull and the water will gush down—and then stop when the cistern has emptied.

Top Tip

Don't be old-fashioned! Use toilet paper instead of old-style leaves, wastepaper, or rags. The first factory-made toilet paper has just been produced (1857), in the United States.

NEAT AND SWEET. With its cistern fixed high on the wall, this toilet is easy to keep clean. You can reach right around the bowl to scrub or dust, and its shiny glaze (glasslike surface) is durable and hygienic.

OUT OF SIGHT? Some people prefer a commode, where the bowl is hidden inside an armchair. But commodes don't flush. That's the trade off!

25

Spending a Penny

By the early 19th century, most "respectable" people no longer used streets as toilets. Although a man could always visit a bar with a backyard privy, there were few other places to go. Then—what a relief!—in 1834, French engineers invented the first pissoirs (public urinals), for men only. Soon after, they also designed the first public toilets for women. Known politely as "waiting rooms" or "conveniences," these were built in many city streets, railroad stations, and department stores.

Your store is so convenient!

FREE AT LAST! Thanks to public toilets, women could go out all day to shop, work, travel, study, or take part in politics. Before public toilets, they didn't dare to leave their homes for too long.

Now, that's what I call convenient.

French pissoir, 19th century

AROUND 870,000 men and women used the toilets at London's Great Exhibition of 1851. Each person paid a penny to enter, and so going to the toilet became known as "spending a penny"!

How It Works

Traveling on a train or boat or plane? Look out for the vacuum travel toilet! Its motor creates a vacuum that sucks waste away—whoosh!—to a tank for safe storage and disposal later. Vacuum toilets use very little water.

But what about us ladies?

Clean water in

Wastewater out

SIDE BY SIDE. Public toilets for men had rows of urinals. Men stood and faced the wall to use them. Water gushed from pipes to flush the waste away.

Toilets of the Future?

It's a shocking fact that one third of the world's people still do not have access to toilets. One child dies every 20 seconds from diseases spread by sewage. Women can't leave home to work and girls can't go to school because there are no toilets. And poorly designed sewage systems often pollute the environment.

The world needs more toilets and better toilet technology! Since the mid-20th century, engineers have experimented with new designs, from simple compost toilets that work without water to wireless, high-tech "washlets." If you could choose, which type of toilet would be best for you—and for the rest of the world? Would you prefer to design your very own toilet of the future?

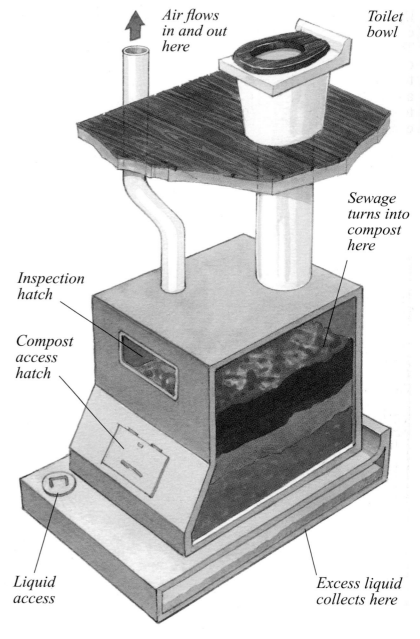

Air flows in and out here

Toilet bowl

Sewage turns into compost here

Inspection hatch

Compost access hatch

Liquid access

Excess liquid collects here

COMPOSTING TOILET
• Sewage drops onto moss, peat, or sawdust.
• Bacteria digest sewage, turning it into hygienic compost.
• Air flows through sewage, helping the bacteria to work.
• Compost needs shaking or stirring, which can be messy!
• Excess liquid gathers at the bottom, which can be smelly!

IN 2001, the United Nations chose November 19 as World Toilet Day. Why? To demand urgent action to bring clean water and clean toilets to everyone, everywhere.

We can't wait!

You Can Do It!

Would you like to live without a toilet? No? You can make a contribution to charities that provide clean water, toilets, and drains to people who do not already have them.

Air purifier

Control panel lets each user program water temperature and spray power

Remote control opens lid and operates flush and body-cleaning water spray

HIGH-TECH TOILET
The first "washlet" (automatic toilet) was made in Japan in 1980. Now there are many designs. Features include:
• Electric power, wireless controls, automatic flush
• Warm seat, massage, air-conditioning
• Water jets for washing, and hot-air dryer, instead of toilet paper
• Checks on user's output, weight, blood pressure

ALREADY, SOME TOILETS pamper their users with perfumes and soft music. What would your ideal future toilet do for you?

Glossary

Ammonia A colorless gas (a mixture of oxygen and hydrogen) with a very strong smell. When mixed with water, it is sometimes used for cleaning.

Bacteria Tiny living organisms, too small to see. They can be useful, harmless, or dangerous to humans.

Cesspit or **cesspool** A hole in the ground used to store sewage.

Chamber pot A bowl used as a toilet, kept in a bedroom or other room. Also known as a potty.

Cholera A dangerous disease caused by bacteria carried in water polluted by sewage.

Cistern Part of a toilet; a tank for storing water.

Closestool A bowl used as a toilet, hidden inside a box or stool.

Commode A bowl used as a toilet, hidden inside a chair.

Compost The rotted remains of plants, combined with other waste. After these have been digested by bacteria, the resulting mixture can be used as garden fertilizer.

Compost toilet or **composting toilet** A toilet without water that uses peat or sawdust to absorb sewage. Bacteria then digest these to produce compost.

Ecosystem A community of plants, animals, and other living things that all depend on each other to survive.

Epidemic A mass outbreak of disease.

Feces Poop—solid waste, produced by humans and other animals.

Float ball A device to control the amount of water flowing into a tank (see diagram at front of book).

Garderobe (or wardrobe) A room or cabinet for storing clothes; also a polite medieval term for a toilet.

Glaze A hard, shiny, glasslike surface on pottery.

Gong farmer A worker who emptied cesspits and carried the sewage away.

Hygienic Clean and healthy.

Miasmas Foul smells. In the past, people thought they caused disease.

Midden A heap of waste or garbage.

Pattens Slip-on shoes with very thick wooden soles, used to keep feet clean and dry.

Pigsty A small yard or pen with a shelter, used to keep pigs.

Pissoir A public toilet for men, designed in France. It contained urinals hidden behind a screen.

Polluted Mixed with poisonous or dangerous substances.

Sewage Waste from toilets; water plus urine and feces.

Sewer A large pipe to carry sewage.

Siphon A pipe or tube shaped like an upside-down U. When liquid flows out from one end of a siphon, the pressure of air outside the tube forces water to flow along it, even uphill.

Trap In toilets, a pipe filled with water that stops smells from rising out of the drains into bathrooms.

Urinal A small toilet for urine only, used by men and boys.

Urine Pee—liquid waste produced by humans and animals.

Water main A large pipe carrying clean water underground.

Index

Toilet Talk

In many cultures, it's still not polite to talk about toilets in public. So if you've really got to go, and you need to ask where, what do you call a toilet? In the past, just like today, people used many different names. Some were clear and easy to understand. Others were more mysterious. Here are just a few, old and new. Those marked * are polite. Be careful with some of the others!

backhouse (England, ca. 1600)
*bathroom (worldwide)
bog (UK, slang)
cloakroom (UK, 19th–20th centuries)
*comfort stop (U.S.)
convenience (UK, 19th century)
dunny (Australia, slang)
garderobe (medieval Europe)
*gents/gentlemen (UK, 19th century)
*hammam (= bathroom, Arabic)
heads (on ships)
house of office (England, 17th century)
john (U.S.)
khazi (British army slang)

*ladies' room (UK and U.S.) or ladies (UK)
latrine (military)
lavatory or lav (from medieval Latin = washroom)
little house (UK)
loo (UK, 20th century)
*men's room (U.S.)
necessary house (England and America, 16th century)
outhouse (U.S., 18th–20th centuries)
*place of convenience (Japan)
place of easement (England, 17th century)
powder room (U.S. and Japan)
privy (UK, ca. 1400–1900)
restroom, retiring room (originally UK, 19th–20th centuries)
*sanitation facility (government offices worldwide)
smallest room (UK)
thatched cottage (China, countryside)
throne (UK, slang)
thunderbox (slang: India, Australia)
*toilet (French, now worldwide)
*water closet or WC (originally English, now worldwide)

Top Toilet Traditions

- Western-style sit-down toilets are unpopular in many parts of Africa and Asia, where traditional squat toilets are still preferred. And many people prefer to clean themselves with water from a bucket or spray, rather than paper.

- In traditional Japanese homes, family and guests put on special slippers to go to the bathroom. They do this to avoid spreading germs and "uncleanness" through other rooms in the house.

- Ships' toilets became known as heads because they were traditionally placed at the bow (front or head) of the ship. As the ship sailed along, waves splashed over the heads and washed them clean.

- Among the Tedong people of Malaysia, it was traditional for a newly married bride and groom not to go to the bathroom for 72 hours after the wedding. This was said to bring good luck.

- In Korea, it has become traditional to give toilet paper to anyone moving to a new home. It is useful (of course!) but also sends a wish that lives in the new home will "unroll" smoothly and happily.

- According to Muslim tradition, it is best to enter a toilet with the left foot, and wipe yourself with your left hand. You should leave a toilet with your right foot forward.

Did You Know?

- Around 1860, British plumber Thomas Crapper invented a toilet seat fitted with a powerful spring. Users could pull it down to sit on, but when they stood up it snapped back (all too quickly!) into an upright position. After several unfortunate accidents to his customers, Crapper stopped selling it.

- When you flush a toilet, bacteria sprayed into the air can travel 6 feet (1.8 meters), and stay active for up to two hours.

- When toilet paper was first sold in shops, many women were too embarrassed to mention it by name. They asked for "curling papers" (used to create fancy hairstyles), instead. The shop assistants understood.

- There is a museum dedicated to decorated toilet seats in San Antonio, Texas.

- Artificial Christmas trees were invented in 1930 by a company that made brushes for cleaning toilets. Aside from the color, the tree branches and the brushes looked very similar, and were manufactured in the same way.

- In Japan, an urban myth tells of Hanako-san, the bathroom ghost. She haunts school bathrooms, banging doors and scaring anyone brave enough to enter.